Better Together

LEADER'S COMPANION

THE DAILY GRACE CO.

Contents

How to use this resource

Our hope and prayer for this leader's companion is that it would be used as a tool to help establish and guide a discipling relationship between two individuals or in the context of a small group. If you have purchased this leader guide companion, it is intended to be used by a designated leader to facilitate and structure the time spent working through *Better Together: A Guide for Discipleship*. The first thing to consider is initiating a discipling relationship with someone you hope to grow alongside. Initiating could be as simple as approaching someone at church, taking someone out for coffee, bringing it up in conversation, or simply calling the person up with an invitation to walk through this resource with you in hopes that you can grow in godliness together. If you do not already have someone in mind, begin praying and thinking of who you would like to ask to join you.

The content of this resource includes how to lead and facilitate *Better Together: A Guide for Discipleship*, with an emphasis on how to set expectations, encourage and exhort, offer accountability, give wise counsel, and ask intentional questions. The intention would be to use this leader companion as you move through each week of *Better Together: A Guide for Discipleship* together as quickly or as slowly as you would like. The ultimate goal of discipleship is that Christians would utilize these types of relationships to flourish in the faith, love God more, and in turn, seek to glorify Him with their lives. We hope this resource equips you in this way!

LEADER'S ROLE

Your greatest role in facilitating the discipleship resource is remaining committed and faithful to God's Word.

If you are reading this companion, you have likely taken the initiative to lead or facilitate working through *Better Together: A Guide for Discipleship*. But you may be unsure of what this role will look like. It is important to have a clear idea of how to best lead and communicate well with those who join you in walking through *Better Together: A Guide for Discipleship*.

Your greatest role in facilitating the discipleship resource is remaining committed and faithful to God's Word. This is the most important thing about the way we lead, teach, and instruct. It safeguards us against speaking falsely about something and additionally, emboldens us with the authority to speak truth into the life of another. Before we guide others in their understanding of God's Word, we must first let it shape our own hearts and minds.

It can be helpful to read and study the passages you will cover prior to the time you meet together. This also helps your familiarity with the subject matter when any questions or confusion arise. Always refer to Scripture to answer questions about Scripture, and embrace the humble response, "I don't know. Let's look into that together," when you are unsure about an answer. When presented with passages to look over in a section, do not skip over them, but make time to read and discuss. As you learn and grow together, remember that God is always teaching us through His Word. Model the impact it has on your own life by leaning into the truth it provides, serving as an example to those you lead.

In the role of leading, you commit yourself to help one another grow in his or her faith. This is an intentional role that holds great impact. You are provided with an opportunity to live in such a faithful and godly way that it can be reproduced in the lives of those who look up to you. This means that your life should exemplify the truths you proclaim, even outside of your time meeting together. Use every opportunity to lead by example.

Come to each discipleship meeting prepared. Complete reading and workbook assignments, memorize Scripture, and answer any questions. Your partner will be encouraged to come prepared, knowing you too are invested. Ask your partner for prayer requests related to daily life and spiritual growth, and pray together at your meeting. Speak words of affirmation when your discipleship partner makes connections to Scripture, completes the assigned study work, memorizes Scripture, or speaks honestly about struggles. Look for opportunities to comment on growth, and in humility, be truthful about areas where he or she might be straying from Scripture and wandering into sin. Your discipleship partner needs honesty wrapped in love, not flattery.

Whether you are meeting with a discipleship partner weekly or monthly, it can be easy to lose touch between meetings. Out of sight should not mean out of mind in a discipleship relationship, so one of the most helpful things you can do for your partner is to remain in touch between meetings. Handwriting a letter goes a long way in a tech-heavy culture, but you can also send an encouraging text during the week, or write an email with Scriptures exhorting your partner in perseverance. Set a reminder on your phone to check in between meetings to let him or her know you are praying over the shared requests. Invite those you lead into your life and home. Think of ways to bring them along in your efforts to show hospitality, to evangelize, and to serve in the ministry of your local church. Often the most valuable way for others to see how to walk faithfully with God is to witness it in the lives of those with whom they are nearest.

Of most importance is the commitment to continually pray for the individual and your time together. Write down requests—the small and the bold, and actually seek God in prayer for them. You can do this together in preparation for the time or following the time and in your personal prayer life. This helps you and those you lead to hearts positioned with the understanding that spiritual growth ultimately comes from the Lord at work in us, not from our own doing. In that regard, we can praise God when we see Him at work. Likewise, we can ask for His help when we see an area of weakness in our own lives or in the lives of those we lead.

"

YOUR LIFE SHOULD EXEMPLIFY THE TRUTHS YOU PROCLAIM, EVEN OUTSIDE OF YOUR TIME MEETING TOGETHER.

NOTES

SETTING EXPECTATIONS

*The fruit of our commitment is more than worth it, and
the growth that takes place prepares us for heaven.*

It is important to discuss expectations as you walk through this resource alongside those you are leading. By discussing expectations for your relationship, you can avoid the gray area and confusion of unmet expectations. Take some time initially to discuss what you expect in your discipleship relationship. Think through what your time will look like, where you will meet, how long you will meet, when you will meet, and your level of commitment. It can be helpful to pick a certain day of the week for consistency or choose up to six dates to put in the calendar to ensure that too much time does not pass between meetings.

In the discipleship resource, you will walk through a section on expectations that will help you best facilitate the conversation. Set a foundation for your commitment to one another, rooted in an unbending devotion to God's Word, prayer, and partnership in the work of the gospel. You can encourage and emphasize these foundational elements by spending the bulk of your time reading God's Word and praying together.

Do your best to keep the conversation intentionally focused on the weekly elements. At times, we can easily drift into side tangents or struggle to move on from the small talk. By beginning and ending your time with prayer, you can help properly posture your hearts and minds while having a start and end to the time. It is also helpful to encourage a handheld Bible instead of a phone or iPad. This helps to curb any possible distractions that can arise during your meeting times and provides natural familiarity with the Scriptures while flipping through the pages and seeing where each verse, passage, chapter, or book is located.

Lastly, our hope is that these relationships would encourage obedience and steadfastness in the faith. Our aim is not only to connect during our scheduled times together but to invest deeply in the lives of one another. Think purposefully of ways to initiate with those you are leading outside of your scheduled time together, whether that means catching up after church, bringing a meal, or even something as simple as making a phone call to check in. The more we step into each other's lives, the more difficult it is to be inconsistent or to hide things from one another. We must be willing to get down in the trenches to speak truth to one another when life is hard, and God's Word seems to fall flat on our ears. We must choose to be gracious and compassionate when expectations change, and our relationships take a new shape. Discipleship is not always easy—it can seem like hard work at times, but the fruit of our commitment is more than worth it, and the growth that takes place prepares us for heaven.

❝

OUR AIM IS NOT ONLY TO CONNECT
DURING OUR SCHEDULED TIMES TOGETHER
BUT TO INVEST DEEPLY IN THE LIVES
OF ONE ANOTHER.

NOTES

ENCOURAGING & EXHORTING

Encouragement among believers is vital to our avoidance of sin and our perseverance in the faith.

Discipleship relationships have the potential to blossom into deep, meaningful friendships that produce mutual encouragement for flourishing in the faith. While those relationships usually begin with much fervor and excitement, remaining invested can be a struggle when the newness wears off. Our discipleship partners will benefit from regular encouragement and exhortation to continue in the relationship, so our role as leaders is more than simply teaching.

The words "encourage" and "exhort" are used often in Scripture, sometimes interchangeably. To understand the proper place of encouragement and exhortation in a discipleship relationship, we will define these terms so that we are equipped to use both of them in spurring on our partners to follow Christ.

ENCOURAGEMENT

To encourage means to stimulate by assistance or approval and to inspire with courage, spirit, or confidence. Encouragement nudges us to do something difficult or stirs up a renewed fervor when we are struggling. A discipleship relationship should communicate a spirit of care and camaraderie, as if to say, "I love you, and I am in this with you!" Coming alongside your discipleship partner will be more effective than simply giving direction to complete study tasks. Using encouragement will move you from teacher to companion, which will help the other person feel like you are both growing in faith together. Your discipleship partner will learn from you what encouragement looks like and will likely reciprocate.

We are commanded in Hebrews to practice encouragement daily in order to help other believers avoid sin and hold fast to Christ. The author of Hebrews 3:13 says, "But encourage each other daily, while it is still called today, so that none of you is hardened by sin's deception." Encouragement is not just a positive way to say something; encouragement among believers is vital to our avoidance of sin and our perseverance in the faith.

EXHORTATION

To exhort means to urge, advise or caution earnestly, or to admonish urgently. If "exhort" sounds like a more serious word, that is because it is. In an exhortation, there is urgency behind our words and actions. When the stakes are high, exhortation communicates both correction and warning. While this might seem a bit harsh for a discipleship relationship, we all need to be earnestly advised to continue in the faith at times. We are easily distracted and can become flippant about sin. Exhortation to stay on the path of perseverance should communicate concern as well as caution and must always be given in love rather than judgment.

Paul tells us, "Let the word of Christ dwell richly among you, in all wisdom teaching and admonishing one another through psalms, hymns, and spiritual songs, singing to God with gratitude in your hearts" (Colossians 3:16). We can exhort others through the use of Scripture, humbly correcting error and pointing to the truth of God's Word as the foundation for our faithfulness.

When exhorting in your discipling relationship, seek to provide biblical truth that will let your partner know you have done so out of love and are invested in his or her spiritual growth.

Because we live in a world full of distractions, suffering, and sinful temptations, we need stirring up in the faith, inspiration to press on, and admonishment reminding us how much perseverance matters. We need both encouragement and exhortation to keep following Jesus "while it is still called today" (Hebrews 3:13).

ENCOURAGEMENT AND EXHORTATION IN ACTION

Some of the challenges in discipleship relationships may include canceled meetings, contact limited to only those meetings, and hesitancy to be transparent. As a person in a leadership role, you might feel discouraged when some of these challenges arise in your discipleship relationship. Remember, though, that exhortation and encouragement are gifts from the Lord that can help overcome some of these difficulties. You will be a blessing to your discipleship partner when you connect both during your meetings and outside of them.

You can probably remember classes in school when the teachers merely lectured and dictated assignments. But what was likely more effective in your perseverance in academics were the classes where the teachers were interested in your life, encouraged you in your work, affirmed your successes, and coupled their corrections with help. Similarly, your discipleship partnership will flourish when you view your role as an exhorter and encourager—as one who comes alongside the other partner as you both walk with Christ.

_____

_____

_____

_____

_____

_____

_____

_____

_____

_____

_____

_____

_____

_____

_____

_____

"

DISCIPLESHIP RELATIONSHIPS HAVE THE
POTENTIAL TO BLOSSOM INTO DEEP,
MEANINGFUL FRIENDSHIPS THAT PRODUCE
MUTUAL ENCOURAGEMENT FOR
FLOURISHING IN THE FAITH.

WISE COUNSEL

*Wise counsel is guidance and advice that comes
from the truth of Scripture.*

Much help and wisdom can be found in a discipleship relationship. Wise counsel from others should be a way of life for us. We will never outgrow a need for counsel from others. We know that wise counsel is important because it is continuously repeated in Scripture. The wisdom literature of Proverbs alone is filled with wisdom for receiving wise counsel:

- *"let a wise person listen and increase learning, and let a discerning person obtain guidance" (Proverbs 1:5)*

- *"Without guidance, a people will fall, but with many counselors there is deliverance." (Proverbs 11:14)*

- *"A fool's way is right in his own eyes, but whoever listens to counsel is wise." (Proverbs 12:15)*

- *"Arrogance leads to nothing but strife, but wisdom is gained by those who take advice." (Proverbs 13:10)*

- *"Plans fail when there is no counsel, but with many advisers they succeed." (Proverbs 15:22)*

- *"Listen to counsel and receive instruction so that you may be wise later in life. Many plans are in a person's heart, but the Lord's decree will prevail." (Proverbs 19:20-21)*

- *"for you should wage war with sound guidance—victory comes with many counselors." (Proverbs 24:6)*

When we surround ourselves with people who will speak truthfully into our lives, we are kept safe from making unwise decisions. Wise counsel is guidance and advice that comes from the truth of Scripture. God is the beginning of wisdom, and there is nothing in and of ourselves or anyone else that gives wisdom apart from God. As Proverbs 9:10 tells us, "The fear of the Lord is the beginning of wisdom, and the knowledge of the Holy One is understanding."

It is likely that those you are leading will not only have questions about this study but also questions about life and personal things they are going through. Telling someone what he or she wants to hear is not wise counsel. Refraining from calling out sin in someone's life is not wise counsel. Giving your opinions and counsel based on your own ideas and experiences apart from what the Bible says is not wise counsel. Take advantage of the opportunity when questions and confusion arise to teach and counsel with both wisdom and discernment found in God's Word. Look to Scripture first for answers and instructions that are clearly provided. If there are gray areas, aim to provide godly counsel that ultimately encourages those you lead to trust in the Lord and lean on Him for understanding. You do not want the person you are discipling to see you as the source of answers for all questions. Instead, you want to help point and equip him or her to seek God and His Word for the answers to questions that arise.

NOTES

66

GOD IS THE BEGINNING OF WISDOM.

ACCOUNTABILITY

We are best equipped to pursue godliness when we humbly and vulnerably invite others into our lives to help us along the way.

For continuous growth and change, we need others to hold us accountable for what we say and do. Understanding accountability stems from the realization that we must answer and give an account to God for our actions in life (Romans 2:15-16, 2 Corinthians 5:10), and we are best equipped to pursue godliness when we humbly and vulnerably invite others into our lives to help us along the way (Hebrews 10:23-24). Accountability helps to safeguard us from falling back into old patterns, bad habits, or common sin struggles. James 5:16 says, "Therefore, confess your sins to one another and pray for one another…," and Galatians 6:1 adds the additional instruction, "if someone is overtaken in any wrongdoing, you who are spiritual, restore such a person with a gentle spirit, watching out for yourselves so that you also won't be tempted." This is a command to us as Christians—as brothers and sisters—to fight against sin together and to bear one another's burdens (Galatians 6:2).

Accountability is vital to our growth as Christians and a necessary element of discipleship. As you lead others through this resource, it is important to model honesty and vulnerability. Confess your sin, share your struggles, and ask to be held accountable just as you would expect from those you are leading. Carve out space at the beginning or end of your meeting to share your lives with one another, and ask the tough questions.

Provided in the discipleship resource is a list of questions (shown on the next page) to walk through together. Reference a few of the following questions each time you meet together. Use this as an opportunity to encourage an honest assessment of your lives. Make sure to write down responses so you are best equipped to follow up, and ask questions in future meetings.

☐ *Have you spent adequate time in Bible study and prayer?*

☐ *What is God teaching you through the study of His Word?*

☐ *How has your prayer life been shaping you?*

☐ *Is there sin you need to confess?*

☐ *Is there forgiveness you need to seek out?*

☐ *How have you seen God's sanctifying work in your life?*

☐ *What spiritual conversations have you had this week?*

☐ *Are you stewarding your time and resources well?*

☐ *How have you been honoring and loving to those closest to you?*

☐ *Have you been faithful in the ministry entrusted to you?*

"

ACCOUNTABILITY IS VITAL TO OUR GROWTH AS CHRISTIANS AND A NECESSARY ELEMENT OF DISCIPLESHIP.

NOTES

GETTING DEEPER

We want to equip and encourage those we lead to look
to God's Word for help and understanding.

A discipleship relationship should possess a level of depth to ensure that you are making the most of your time together. This does not always come naturally or with ease in the beginning, especially if you are still getting to know someone. We grow in depth and understanding of others when we feel they truly care for us, and in turn, we begin to trust them more. Initially, there may be a feeling of surface-level conversation and answers. Initiate in ways that aim to take things beyond the surface by asking open-ended questions. You can respond to a yes or no answer with a question that seeks to draw out more of a response. You can respond to a vague answer with, "Can you tell me a little more about that?" Think about how to stretch the depth of your relationship by asking intentional follow-up questions.

At times, there may even be awkward silences or uncomfortable questions. Do not avoid them, but embrace them. Allow for time to think and wrestle with thoughts. Encourage those you are leading along when you notice them struggling to respond, or suggest looking at a passage of Scripture together. As mentioned previously, we do not want to spoon-feed answers, but instead, we want to equip and encourage those we lead to look to God's Word for help and understanding. This is of great importance in our lives as Christians and our lives beyond these discipleship relationships.

As the discipleship leader, it is important that your motives are purely out of love, care, and a true desire to equip and encourage those you lead. Seek to be understanding, getting to know those you disciple as image-bearing individuals created uniquely and wonderfully. Proverbs 20:5 reminds us, "Counsel in a person's heart is deep water, but a person of understanding draws it out." Be patient and gracious, fighting against the temptation to lead with a one-size-fits-all mentality. Pray, and ask God to give you those desires and equip and sustain in you a tender and compassionate heart for those you lead to better create space for deeper and lasting growth together.

“

WE GROW IN DEPTH AND UNDERSTANDING
OF OTHERS WHEN WE FEEL THEY TRULY
CARE FOR US, AND IN TURN, WE BEGIN
TO TRUST THEM MORE.

NOTES

THE END GOAL

We engage in discipleship because we want to see our fellow image-bearers grow in their love and knowledge of God.

The end goal of life is to glorify God and enjoy Him forever. This goal is the same for our discipleship relationships as well. We engage in discipleship because we want to see our fellow image-bearers grow in their love and knowledge of God. We know from personal experience that this kind of spiritual growth will increase their joy and delight in God and in turn, cause them to lead lives glorifying to Him. That is our aim in our personal lives and in our discipling efforts—to see God glorified and enjoyed by all people groups.

The beauty of God's economy is that as we invest in the spiritual growth of others for the glory of God, we grow in spiritual maturity and better glorify Him as well. We see an upside-down nature to God's kingdom throughout Scripture. We find that as we empty ourselves, we are filled with Christ. As we take up our crosses, we experience abundant life. As we serve others out of humble reverence to God, we are promised to be exalted (Matthew 23:11-12). As leaders, we are to emulate Christ in our thoughts, words, and deeds. We are to proclaim the excellencies of Christ in our spheres of influence, not because piety or religiosity will garner us favor with God but because of our identities in Him. In Christ, we are part of a royal priesthood, called out of darkness "into His marvelous light" so that we may proclaim His praises (1 Peter 2:9). This is the heart of discipleship—to see others find their identities in Christ, to help them live in light of their identities in Him, and to link arms in proclaiming His praises.

Our love for God compels our obedience to His command to make disciples. However, the glorious reality is that our obedience to Him deepens our love for Him. The end goal of being discipled and discipling others is to see more and more people grow in their love and knowledge of God and have lives transformed in response—all to the praise of His glory.

"

THE BEAUTY OF GOD'S ECONOMY IS
THAT AS WE INVEST IN THE SPIRITUAL
GROWTH OF OTHERS FOR THE GLORY OF GOD,
WE GROW IN SPIRITUAL MATURITY AND
BETTER GLORIFY HIM AS WELL.

NOTES

PRAYERS FOR YOUR
DISCIPLESHIP RELATIONSHIP

It is a joy and a privilege to disciple someone. As we lead others to grow in Christ-likeness, we remember that only God can change hearts and produce lasting fruit. For this reason, we must pray over those we disciple, asking that God would capture their affections and work redemptively in their lives.

Use the following prayer prompts to pray over the person you are discipling this week. Occasionally, text her and let her know that you are praying for her.

1. Pray that she would love the Lord with all her heart, soul, mind, and strength. Pray that she would grow in grace and surrender her life to the Lord daily.

2. Pray that she would grow in her love for God's Word and have the discipline to study the Bible daily. Pray that she would renew her mind with Scripture more often than turn to TV, blog posts, or other books.

3. Pray that she would grow in her prayer life. Pray that she would go to the Lord as her refuge in times of joy and hardship.

4. Spend time praying for any sin struggles she has shared with you. Pray for her holiness, purity, and self-control. Pray that she would bring any hidden sins into the light and that she would continue to grow in Christlikeness.

5. Pray for deep friendships with other believers in her local church. Pray that her family and work relationships would flourish with grace, love, and good communication. Pray that she would seek meaningful relationships filled with accountability and fellowship.

6. Pray that she would be bold in sharing the gospel with others. Pray for evangelistic opportunities and the courage to share her faith with family, friends, and neighbors.

7. Pray that she would grow in humility, wisdom, and servant-heartedness. Pray that she would be open and teachable during your time together.

8. Pray that she would steward her time well. Pray that she would balance work, relationships, hobbies, and rest in a way that honors God.

9. Pray that she would cultivate strong character, growing in truthfulness and integrity.

10. Pray that she would have contentment and joy in the Lord, no matter the season of life.

PRAYER LOG

DATE: ___ / ___ / ___

PRAYER REQUEST: _____
_____
_____
_____

HOW I AM SEEING GOD WORK: _____
_____
_____

DATE: ___ / ___ / ___

PRAYER REQUEST: _____
_____
_____
_____

HOW I AM SEEING GOD WORK: _____
_____
_____

DATE: ___ / ___ / ___

PRAYER REQUEST: _____
_____
_____
_____

HOW I AM SEEING GOD WORK: _____
_____
_____

DATE: ___ / ___ / ___

PRAYER REQUEST: _____

_____

_____

_____

HOW I AM SEEING GOD WORK: _____

_____

_____

DATE: ___ / ___ / ___

PRAYER REQUEST: _____

_____

_____

_____

HOW I AM SEEING GOD WORK: _____

_____

_____

DATE: ___ / ___ / ___

PRAYER REQUEST: _____

_____

_____

_____

HOW I AM SEEING GOD WORK: _____

_____

_____

DATE: / /

PRAYER REQUEST: _____

_____

_____

_____

HOW I AM SEEING GOD WORK: _____

_____

_____

DATE: / /

PRAYER REQUEST: _____

_____

_____

_____

HOW I AM SEEING GOD WORK: _____

_____

_____

DATE: / /

PRAYER REQUEST: _____

_____

_____

_____

HOW I AM SEEING GOD WORK: _____

_____

_____

DATE: / /

PRAYER REQUEST: _____

_____

_____

_____

HOW I AM SEEING GOD WORK: _____

_____

_____

DATE: / /

PRAYER REQUEST: _____

_____

_____

_____

HOW I AM SEEING GOD WORK: _____

_____

_____

DATE: / /

PRAYER REQUEST: _____

_____

_____

_____

HOW I AM SEEING GOD WORK: _____

_____

_____

DATE: / /

PRAYER REQUEST: _____

_____

_____

_____

HOW I AM SEEING GOD WORK: _____

_____

_____

DATE: / /

PRAYER REQUEST: _____

_____

_____

_____

HOW I AM SEEING GOD WORK: _____

_____

_____

DATE: / /

PRAYER REQUEST: _____

_____

_____

_____

HOW I AM SEEING GOD WORK: _____

_____

_____

DATE: ___ / ___ / ___

PRAYER REQUEST: _____

_____

_____

_____

HOW I AM SEEING GOD WORK: _____

_____

_____

DATE: ___ / ___ / ___

PRAYER REQUEST: _____

_____

_____

_____

HOW I AM SEEING GOD WORK: _____

_____

_____

DATE: ___ / ___ / ___

PRAYER REQUEST: _____

_____

_____

_____

HOW I AM SEEING GOD WORK: _____

_____

_____

DATE: / /

PRAYER REQUEST: _____

_____

_____

_____

HOW I AM SEEING GOD WORK: _____

_____

_____

DATE: / /

PRAYER REQUEST: _____

_____

_____

_____

HOW I AM SEEING GOD WORK: _____

_____

_____

DATE: / /

PRAYER REQUEST: _____

_____

_____

_____

HOW I AM SEEING GOD WORK: _____

_____

_____

DATE: __ / __ / __

PRAYER REQUEST: _____

_____

_____

_____

HOW I AM SEEING GOD WORK: _____

_____

_____

DATE: __ / __ / __

PRAYER REQUEST: _____

_____

_____

_____

HOW I AM SEEING GOD WORK: _____

_____

_____

DATE: __ / __ / __

PRAYER REQUEST: _____

_____

_____

_____

HOW I AM SEEING GOD WORK: _____

_____

_____

Thank you for studying
God's Word with us!

CONNECT WITH US
@thedailygraceco
@kristinschmucker

CONTACT US
info@thedailygraceco.com

SHARE
#thedailygraceco
#lampandlight

VISIT US ONLINE
thedailygraceco.com

MORE DAILY GRACE
The Daily Grace App
Daily Grace Podcast